Cool
HOLIDAY
FOOD ART

Easy Recipes That Make Food Fun to Eat!

Nancy Tuminelly

ABDO
Publishing Company

To Adult Helpers

This is not your ordinary cookbook! Sure, we've provided ingredients lists and how-to photographs. But like any artistic endeavor, food art is all about creativity! Encourage kids to come up with their own ideas. Get creative with ingredients too. Scan your fridge and get started with whatever you have!

Always supervise kids when they are working in the kitchen. Food art often requires a lot of knife work such as slicing and shaping. Assist young artists whenever they are using knives. Occasionally, kids will need to use the oven or stovetop too. Be there to help when necessary, but encourage them to do as much as they can on their own. Kids love to share and eat their own creations!

Expect your young food artists to make a mess, but also expect them to clean up after themselves. Show them how to properly store unused ingredients. Most importantly, be a voice of encouragement. You might even get kids to eat healthy foods they've never had before!

Visit us at www.abdopublishing.com

Published by ABDO Publishing Company, 8000 West 78th Street, Edina, Minnesota 55439. Copyright © 2011 by Abdo Consulting Group, Inc. International copyrights reserved in all countries. No part of this book may be reproduced in any form without written permission from the publisher. Checkerboard Library™ is a trademark and logo of ABDO Publishing Company.

Printed in the United States of America, North Mankato, Minnesota
062010
092010

 PRINTED ON RECYCLED PAPER

Editor: Liz Salzmann
Series Concept: Nancy Tuminelly
Cover and Interior Design: Anders Hanson, Mighty Media, Inc.
Photo Credits: Anders Hanson, Shutterstock

The following manufacturers/names appearing in this book are trademarks: Betty Crocker® Easy Writer™, Betty Crocker® Super Moist®, C&H®, Cake Mate®, India Tree, Karo®, Kraft® Jet-Puffed®, Morton®, Pillsbury® Creamy Supreme®, Wilton® Decorating Icing®

Library of Congress Cataloging-in-Publication Data

Tuminelly, Nancy, 1952-
   Cool holiday food art : easy recipes that make food fun to eat! / Nancy Tuminelly.
      p. cm. -- (Cool food art)
   Includes index.
   ISBN 978-1-61613-365-8
   1. Holiday cookery--Juvenile literature. 2. Food presentation--Juvenile literature. I. Title.
   TX739.T78 2010
   946.9'032--dc22
                            2010003476

CONTENTS

PAGE 16

PAGE 18

PAGE 20

PAGE 26

PLAY WITH YOUR FOOD!

Unless Mom says not to!

It's time to play with your food! Get ready to make turkeys, groundhogs, and monsters. You're an artist now. The plate is your **canvas**, and your favorite foods are your paints!

As you make your holiday food art, be open to all sorts of ingredients. You can use anything! Candies, icing, and sprinkles work really well. You can use them to create just about any **design**!

Like any kind of art, food art is about **expression** and creativity. Get inspired and give each recipe your own special touch. A lot of cookbooks teach you how to make holiday recipes that taste great. This book will inspire you to make holiday treats that taste and look great!

THE BASICS

Get started with a few important basics

ASK PERMISSION

> Before you cook, get permission to use the kitchen, cooking tools, and ingredients.

> You might want an adult to help you with some of your creations. But if you want to do something yourself, say so!

> When you need help, just ask. An adult should always be around when you are using sharp knives, the oven, or the stove.

BE PREPARED

> Read through the recipe before you begin.

> Get organized. Have your tools and ingredients ready before you start.

> Think of **alternative** ingredients if you want!

BE SMART, BE SAFE

> Never work in the kitchen when you are home alone!

> Have an adult nearby when you are using sharp tools such as a knife, peeler, or grater. Always use sharp tools with care. Use a cutting board when you are working with a knife.

> Work slowly and carefully. Great food art rarely happens when you rush!

BE NEAT AND CLEAN

> Start with clean hands, clean tools, and a clean work surface.

> Always wash fruits and vegetables. Rinse them under cold water. Pat them dry with a towel. Then they won't slip when you cut them.

> Tie back long hair so it stays out of the way and out of the food!

> Wear comfortable clothes that can get a little bit dirty. Roll up your sleeves.

Note on Measuring

The recipes in this book provide **approximations**. Feel free to be creative! For example, a recipe may call for 1 tablespoon of cream cheese. Do you like cream cheese? Then add more! If you don't like cream cheese, then try something else!

SHOPPING FOR PRODUCE

Sometimes canned produce works perfectly in your food art. But more often than not, fresh fruits and vegetables are better. When you are shopping for your food art groceries, think about what you are making. For example, do you want a really big pear or a small one? Fruits and vegetables come in all different shapes and sizes! Think about the shapes and sizes that will work best in your food art.

SAVING INGREDIENTS

When you are making food art, sometimes you only need a little bit of something. That means you have to do a good job of putting things away so they stay fresh. Cover leftover ingredients so that they will keep. Airtight containers work best. You don't want to waste a lot of food!

KEY SYMBOLS

In this book, you will see some **symbols** beside the recipes. Here is what they mean.

Sharp!

You need to use a knife for this recipe. Ask an adult to stand by.

Hot!

This activity requires the use of an oven or stove. You need adult supervision. Always use oven mitts when holding hot pans.

THE COOLEST

BUTTER

ASSORTED
CHEESES

HARD-BOILED EGG

MAYONNAISE

MUSTARD

BOSC PEAR

CANTALOUPE

RED APPLE

RED GRAPES

PINEAPPLE
CHUNKS

BELL PEPPERS

GREEN OLIVES WITH
PIMIENTO

SHREDDED
COCONUT

DRIED
CRANBERRIES

CRISPY RICE CEREAL

PRETZELS

LARGE PRETZEL
STICKS

POPCORN

SALT

LIGHT CORN
SYRUP

INGREDIENTS

POWDERED SUGAR

ICING

FROSTING

CAKE MIX

COCOA POWDER

MINI M&MS

CHOCOLATE SYRUP

CHOCOLATE KISSES

COLORED SUGAR CRYSTALS

SPRINKLES

WAFER ICE CREAM CONE

CHOCOLATE SANDWICH COOKIES

MARSHMALLOWS

MINI MARSHMALLOWS

MARSHMALLOW CREME

WHIPPED CREAM

ICE CREAM

FRUIT LEATHER

CANDY CORN

FRUIT CANDY SLICES

GUMDROPS

SPICE DROPS

FOOD COLORING PENS

THE TOOL BOX

Here are some tools you'll need for most food art recipes

LARGE KNIFE

SAUCE PAN

MIXING BOWLS

PARING KNIFE

APPLE CORER

BAKING SHEET

ICING TIPS

ICE CREAM SCOOP

TOOTHPICKS

WAXED PAPER

PLASTIC WRAP

CUTTING BOARD

WOODEN SKEWERS

ROLLING PIN

MEASURING CUPS AND SPOONS

TECHNIQUES

Tips for making great food art

MAKING FACES

Food art is all about creativity. The recipes in this book will get you started. But your imagination is really the secret ingredient! A recipe may call for black olives as the eyes. But why not try raisins instead? Use these techniques for inspiration. Add your personal style to create cool variations!

Eyes

SMALL CANDIES
ON GUMDROPS

GRAPE HALVES ON
MARSHMALLOWS

BLACK OLIVE SLICES
ON CREAM CHEESE

BLUEBERRIES ON
BANANA SLICES

Noses

CANDY CORN

CANTALOUPE BALL

BABY CARROT

RAISIN

Mouths

CANDY FRUIT SLICE

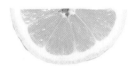

HALF A LEMON SLICE

RED PEPPER TOP

ORANGE SECTION

ATTACHING WITH GOOEY STUFF

Food art combines a variety of ingredients. How do you hold them all together? Ingredients such as peanut butter, mayonnaise, ketchup, and cream cheese can be used like glue. Plus, they taste great!

ATTACHING WITH TOOTHPICKS

When you're making food art, it's a good idea to keep toothpicks handy. You can use them in so many ways! They are great for making small holes in ingredients. Plus, you can use them to hold ingredients together! Just be careful not to bite into them!

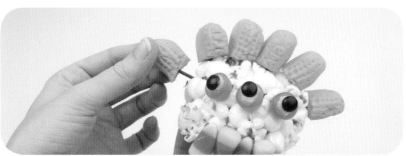

APPLYING ICING

With icing, the possibilities are endless! There are many color choices. There are also many different icing tips that you can use to change the way your icing looks. Here are some of the options and what they do!

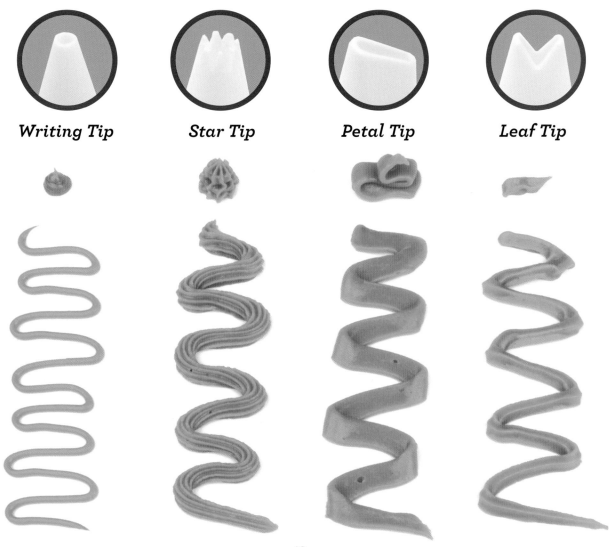

Writing Tip **Star Tip** **Petal Tip** **Leaf Tip**

SUSHI
FOR YOU

A great April Fools' Day trick!

INGREDIENTS

¼ cup butter

4 cups mini marshmallows

6 cups crispy rice cereal

fruit candy slices

1 box green fruit leather

pink gumdrops

green icing

chocolate syrup

TOOLS

baking sheet

wooden spoon

2-quart sauce pan

measuring cups

rolling pin

paring knife

cutting board

1 Grease the baking sheet. Melt the butter in the saucepan over medium heat. Then add the marshmallows. Stir until smooth.

2 Turn the heat to low. Add the rice **cereal**. Stir until mixed.

3 Press the cereal mixture into the baking sheet. You can use a rolling pin to make it more even.

4 Slice the fruit candy into ½-inch (1 cm) strips. Line up about eight candy slices near one end of the baking sheet.

5 Pick up the edge of the cereal mixture and roll it over the fruit candy. Use a knife to cut along the edge of the roll.

6 Repeat steps 4 and 5 until the entire cereal mixture is rolled up.

7 Slice the cereal logs into 1-inch (2.5 cm) rolls. Cut strips of green fruit leather 1 inch (2.5 cm) wide. Wrap the fruit leather strips around the rolls.

8 **Garnish** the plate with sliced pink gumdrops for pickled ginger. Add some green icing for **wasabi**. A bowl of chocolate syrup can be soy sauce.

15

DREIDEL
PRETZEL SNACKS

You'll do more eating than spinning this Hanukkah!

INGREDIENTS

2 large pretzel sticks

4 marshmallows

marshmallow creme

blue sugar crystals

blue food coloring pen

4 chocolate kisses

blue icing

TOOLS

dinner knife

icing tips

1 Break the pretzel sticks in half. Push the broken end of each half into a marshmallow. The pretzel sticks should go almost all the way through the marshmallows.

2 Use a knife to make a thin line of marshmallow creme on the marshmallow. Cover the marshmallow creme line with blue sugar crystals.

3 Repeat step 2 until each marshmallow has four blue lines on it. The lines should be evenly spaced around the marshmallows.

4 Use a blue food coloring pen. Draw one of these Hebrew letters on each side: נ ש ה ג

5 Put a bit of icing on the bottom of each chocolate kiss. Press a chocolate kiss to the bottom of each marshmallow.

6 Put blue icing around the top and bottom of each marshmallow.

17

LITTLE
PEEPERS

These chicks should hatch just before Easter!

INGREDIENTS

3 hard-boiled eggs

2 tablespoons of mayonnaise

¼ teaspoon mustard

⅛ teaspoon salt

orange and yellow bell pepper

3 green olives with pimiento

TOOLS

measuring spoons

apple corer

mixing bowl

fork

paring knife

cutting board

1 Peel the hard-boiled eggs. Cut a thin slice off the bottom of each egg. This is so the eggs will stand up.

2 Cut off the top third of each egg. Save the top for step 7.

3 Carefully scoop out the yolks.

4 Put the yolks in a mixing bowl. Mash them with a fork. Stir in the mayonnaise, mustard, and salt.

5 Fill the empty egg whites with the yolk mixture.

6 Cut six triangles out of a yellow bell pepper for wings. Stick two wings into the egg mixture in each egg. Add a scoop of egg mixture on top of the wings.

7 Slice the olives in half for the eyes. Give each chick a beak made with two small slices of orange bell pepper. Put the top back on each egg.

19

JULY FOURTH
FUN CONES

This treat is independently delicious!

INGREDIENTS

1 scoop ice cream

1 wafer ice cream cone

blue fruit leather

red and blue icing

small white star sprinkles

2 blue mini M&Ms

1 red mini M&M

whipped cream

TOOLS

ice cream scoop

paring knife

cutting board

icing tips

1 Put a round scoop of ice cream on a plate. The scoop should be a little bigger than the top of the cone. Put the plate in the freezer.

2 Cut a strip of fruit leather. It should be as wide as the band at the top of the cone. Wrap the fruit leather around the cone's band.

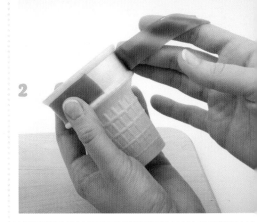

3 Use red icing to make stripes on the cone. Coat the bottom of the cone with blue icing. Put little dabs of blue icing around the cone's band. Stick white star sprinkles to the icing.

4 Take the scoop of ice cream out of the freezer. Turn the cone over and put it on top of the ice cream.

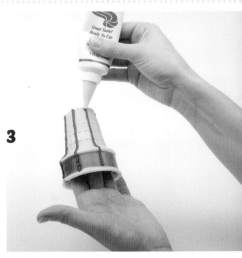

5 Quickly add blue mini M&Ms for the eyes. Use a red mini M&M for the nose.

6 Squirt whipped cream in front of the ice cream face to make a beard.

CREEPY
POPCORN BALLS

Nothing says Halloween like a face with three eyes!

INGREDIENTS

3 tablespoons
light corn syrup

1 tablespoon
butter

½ teaspoon cold
water

¾ cup powdered
sugar

⅓ cup
marshmallows

6 cups popcorn

icing

assorted candy
pieces

TOOLS

measuring
spoons and cups

saucepan

wooden spoon

large bowl

plastic wrap

toothpicks

1 Melt the corn syrup, butter, water, sugar, and marshmallows over medium heat. Stir until the mixture comes to a boil. Add the popcorn and stir well. Put the popcorn mixture in a large bowl.

2 Rub a little butter on your hands. Shape the popcorn mixture into balls while it is still warm. Wrap the balls in plastic wrap and store at room temperature. Unwrap the balls when you are ready to decorate them.

Three-eyed monster

3 Cut two gumdrops in half. Use icing to stick three of the halves to the popcorn ball. Put a dab of icing on each gumdrop. Stick brown mini M&Ms to the icing.

4 Use icing to **attach** candy corns for the mouth.

5 Cut candy peanuts in half. Use toothpicks to attach them to the top of the popcorn ball.

6 Cut two short pieces of a gummy worm. Put them over the eyes for eyebrows.

3

4

5

6

SEE YOUR SHADOW
CUPCAKES

This little groundhog just might be too cute to eat!

INGREDIENTS

2 cake mixes
(make large white
cupcakes and
mini chocolate
cupcakes)

white and
chocolate frosting

1 chocolate
sandwich cookie,
crushed

1 mini
marshmallow

black icing

1 small pink star
sprinkle

2 white sprinkles

4 brown mini
M&Ms

1 spice drop

TOOLS

cutting board

paring knife

icing tips

toothpick

1 Bake the cupcakes according to the directions on the cake mix boxes. Allow them to cool.

2 Cover a white cupcake with white frosting. Sprinkle some chocolate cookie crumbs in the center of the frosting.

3 Cover a mini cupcake with chocolate frosting. Place it on its side on top of the crumbs.

4 Cut the mini marshmallow in half. Stick the halves on the mini cupcake for the eyes. Add a dot of black icing to the center of each eye.

5 Place a small pink sprinkle just below the eyes. Place two white sprinkles just below the pink sprinkle. Use a toothpick to help position them.

6 Put two of the brown mini M&Ms on the face for the cheeks. Put the other two on top of the head for the ears.

7 Cut the spice drop in half lengthwise. Place the halves next to the groundhog's head. They are the front paws.

FRUIT GOBBLE
GOBBLE

Have two kinds of turkey this Thanksgiving!

INGREDIENTS

1 cantaloupe

1 Bosc pear

1 red apple

red grapes

cheese cubes, assorted flavors

pineapple chunks

2 dried cranberries

TOOLS

cutting board

large knife

paring knife

wooden skewers

scissors

toothpicks

1 Cut a thin slice off the large end of the cantaloupe. Set the cantaloupe on a plate.

2 Hold the pear upside down. Use a skewer to **attach** it to the top of the cantaloupe. If the skewer sticks out, cut off the extra with a scissors.

3 Cut a slice off the bottom of the apple. Cut the slice into six small triangle shapes. Arrange the triangles in front of the cantaloupe for the feet.

4 Slice the apple in half. Cut a small slice off of each half. Attach one half of the apple to each side of the cantaloupe. Cut off the skewers if they stick out.

5 Put grapes, cheese cubes, and pineapple chunks on skewers. Push them into the cantaloupe for the tail feathers.

6 Use a toothpick to attach one of the apple slices to the middle of the pear. Put each cranberry on a small pineapple chunk to make eyes. Use toothpicks to attach them to the pear.

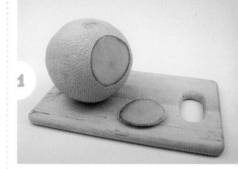

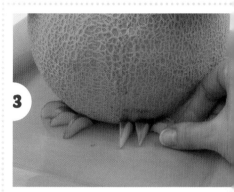

REINDEER
COOKIES

This Rudolph is completely edible. Even his nose!

INGREDIENTS

30 pretzels

¼ cup butter

2 tablespoons cocoa powder

5 cups mini marshmallows

6 cups rice cereal

marshmallow creme

60 brown mini M&Ms

30 red mini M&Ms

pink icing

shredded coconut

TOOLS

waxed paper

2 baking sheets

measuring cups and spoons

2-quart saucepan

wooden spoon

toothpicks

knife

cutting board

icing tips

1 Put the butter, cocoa powder, and 4 cups of mini marshmallows in the saucepan. Put the pan on the stove over low heat. Stir constantly until the marshmallows melt.

2 Add the **cereal** and mix well. Remove from heat. Let the mixture sit until it is cool enough to handle.

3 Rub a little bit of butter on your hands. Make triangle shapes out of the mixture. These are the heads! Set them on baking sheets lined with waxed paper.

4 Use a toothpick to make two small holes in the top of each head. This is easier if the heads are still a bit warm. Break the pretzels in half. Dip the end of each pretzel in marshmallow creme. Stick the pretzels into the holes.

5 Cut 30 mini marshmallows in half. Place two halves on each head for eyes. Use marshmallow creme to **attach** a brown mini M&M to each eye.

6 Use the red M&Ms for noses. Draw the mouths with pink icing. Place each reindeer on a bed of shredded coconut.

WRAP IT UP!

Food art finale!

Now you're ready to **design** your own holiday food art! It helps to have a plan before you start. Make a **sketch** of your idea. Add notes about what ingredients might work best. Talk about your sketch with others. You will get great ideas! Make sure you take photographs before you eat your creations. The better your holiday treats look, the more likely they are to be eaten!

Holidays are great times to give gifts. They are also great times for **celebrating**! You could make some See Your Shadow Cupcakes for your friends, or special holiday treats for a family party. The more you experiment with food art, the more fun you can have!

GLOSSARY

ALTERNATIVE – different from the original.

APPROXIMATION – about the right amount.

ATTACH – to join two things together.

CANVAS – a type of thick cloth that artists paint on.

CELEBRATE – to honor with a party or special ceremony.

CEREAL – a breakfast food usually made from grain and eaten with milk.

DESIGN – 1. a decorative pattern or arrangement. 2. to plan how something will appear or work.

EXPRESSION – creating a work of art as a way to show one's feelings.

GARNISH – to decorate with small amounts of food.

SKETCH – a drawing.

SYMBOL – an object or picture that stands for or represents something.

WASABI – a sauce made from the root of an Asian herb. Wasabi is often served with Japanese food.

Web Sites

INDEX